About the Author

Abdi Aden is a storyteller and author. He loves working with young people. In 2007 Abdi received the Victorian Refugee Recognition Award. Abdi believes that every person has the right to a productive, happy life and that begins with the young people.

'Anything is possible if you try, and try again. I am living proof of that.'

— Abdi

Grandma gives
the best cuddles

Yes, I love and respect
older people...

MY YES I CAN! BOOK

Abdi's Story

ABDI ADEN

ILLUSTRATED BY PAWEL NOWACKI

First published in Australia 2025
by Abdi Aden
Copyright © Abdi Aden 2025

ISBN: 978-0-6481581-2-7

www.facebook.com/inspired.abdi

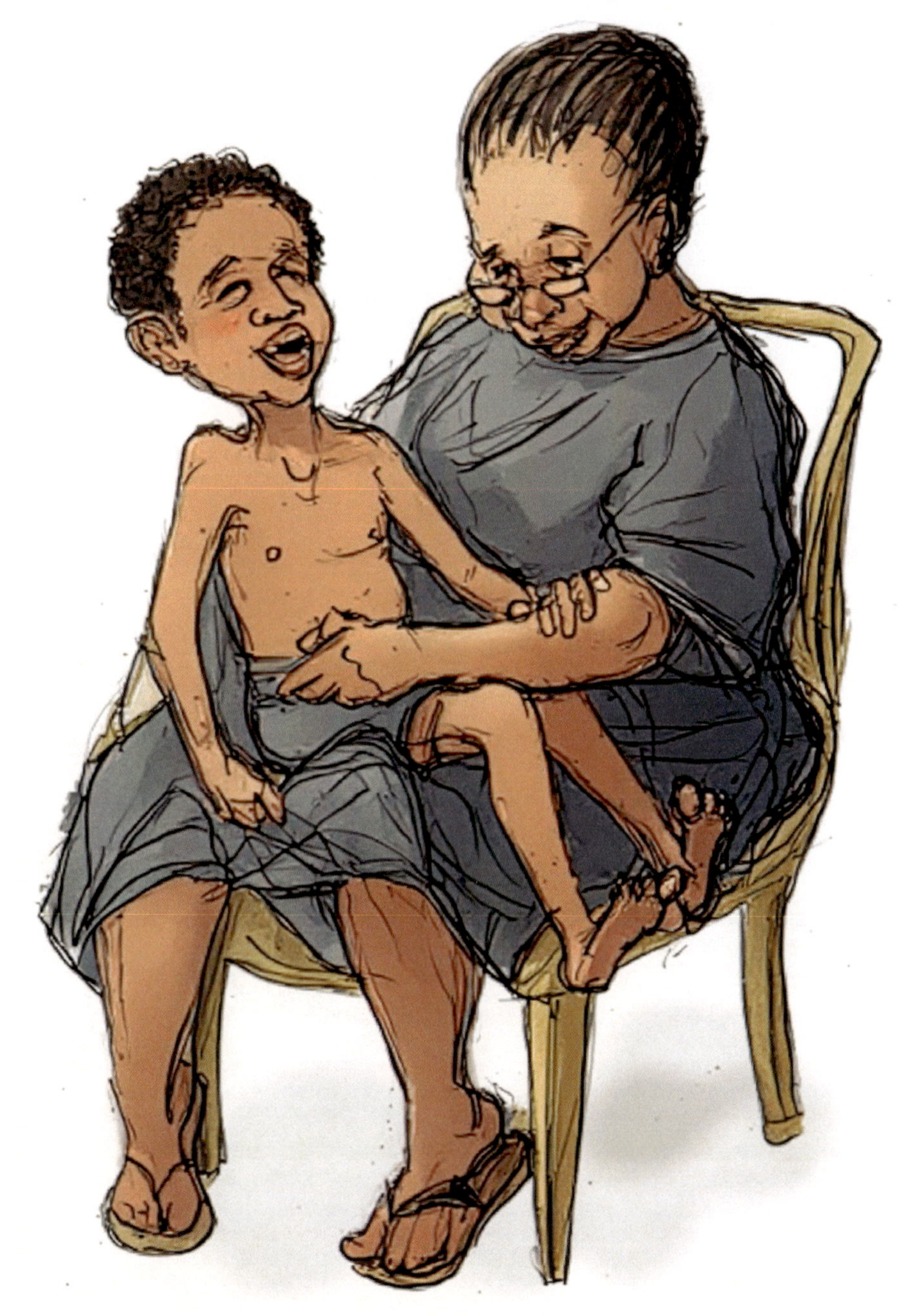

My Best
Friend Aliyow
...Ha, Ha, Ha

I can be a
good friend...

Burying my head in
the sand so I won't
be seen.

I can be silly sometimes...

My sister Jamilia
and also my
superhero

Yes girls, mums,
grandmas, sisters,
aunties are powerful...

Oh no I am in
trouble with Mum

Yes I can learn
when I do
something wrong...

My teacher in Somalia at the beach...how embarrassing

Yes I can learn a lot from my teachers...

Always
dream big

Yes I Can dream
I will play soccer for
Somalia one day...

Yes I Can be
and I will
be great!

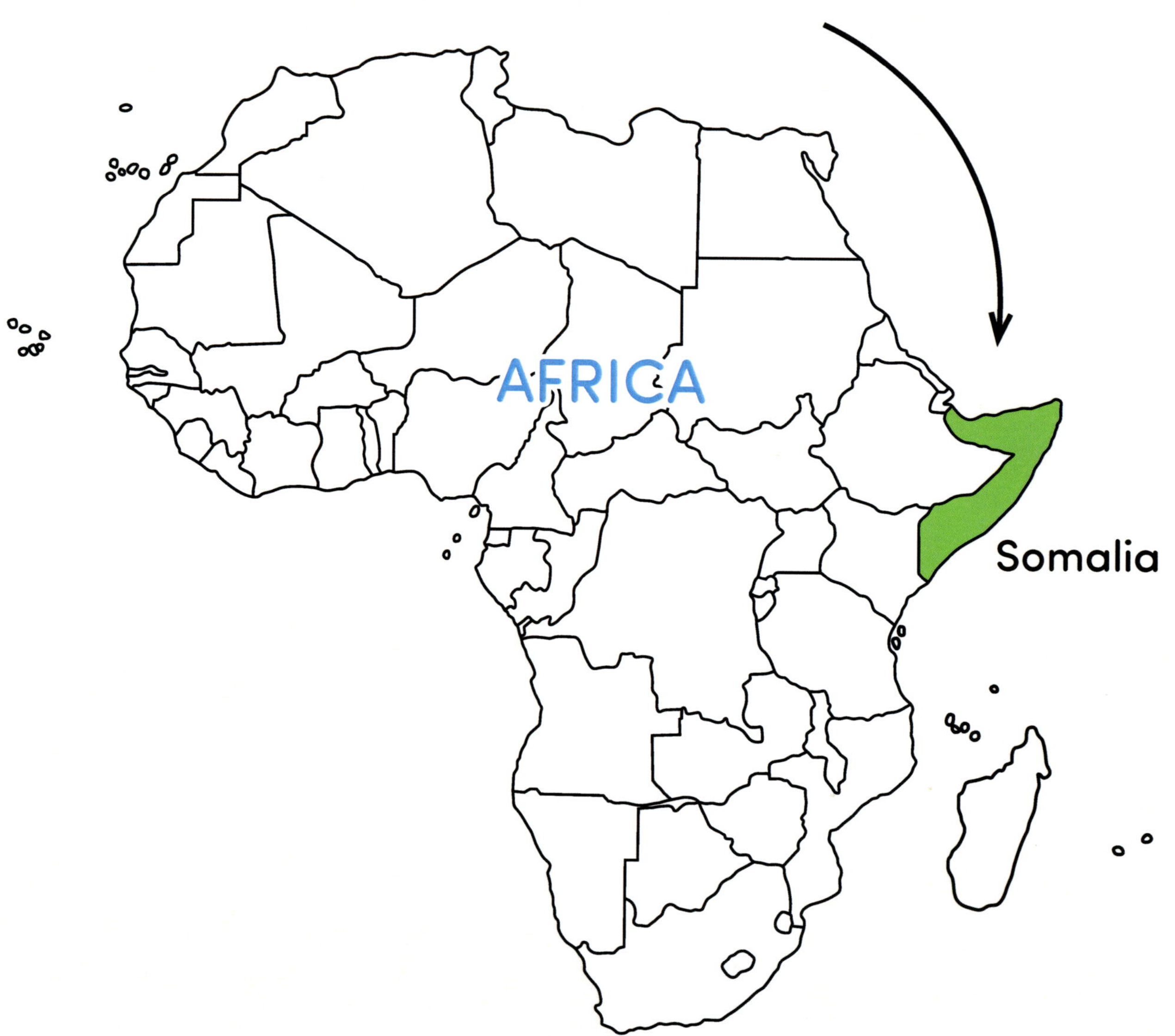

WHERE I WAS BORN
AFRICA
Somalia